STREETdogs

STREETdogs

traer scott

MERRELL

LONDON · NEW YORK

For Liz, Christine, and Benji

Introduction

Todos somos satos WE ARE ALL MUTTS

I encountered the most pitiful stray dog I've ever seen during my honeymoon in Antigua, when we were in a cab returning from a horse-riding excursion. "Marvin" (or Starvin' Marvin, as she was jokingly named by my husband) was an emaciated Chihuahua mix with a distended belly. She was an adult, but so tiny that I mistook her for a puppy. I asked the cabdriver to stop, and when I got out, Marvin came running up to me and jumped into my arms. We took her back to our condo, stuffed her with food until she fell asleep, and then sat there wondering what to do with her. Should we try to fly her back to Boston with us, attempt to find her somewhere safe on the island, or just let her loose on the streets again?

This scenario is repeated all too often with American tourists in the Caribbean and Latin America. There seem to be stray dogs everywhere; some are mangy and starved, but many are puppies or young dogs that were recently someone's pet and are still very approachable. Americans are not used to seeing dogs on the streets. In the United States, the growing stigma associated with animal abandonment, combined with increasingly plentiful alternatives to it, mean that there are very few visible strays. In virtually every city and town, animal control units ensure that any existing stray dogs are picked up immediately, and those that evade capture tend to be feral, quick, and well hidden. Marvin was the first friendly street dog I had seen as an adult. I thought about her often and hoped that the small Humane Society center that I managed to find on the island was able to help her. I had no idea how serious the street dog problem is in many countries, or that there were so many people working ceaselessly to turn the tide.

About four years ago, an article in *Bark* magazine about *satos* caught my eye. *Sato* is Puerto Rican slang for "mutt," although the word has come to be associated with any stray dog, even if it is a purebred. As I read the article while standing in line for groceries, I kept thinking how remarkable it would be to photograph these dogs and bring their faces and their plight to a larger audience. Years later,

Opposite: Jennifer Holmes, director of the San Felipe Animal Rescue in Mexico, is greeted by dogs at the shelter.

thanks largely to the success of my first book, *Shelter Dogs*, I finally got that chance. I spent the early months of 2007 traveling in Puerto Rico and Mexico, working closely with animal rescuers in different cities and villages, people who are striving to make a real difference in the lives of these dogs. Although a street dog problem exists in parts of Italy, Romania, Brazil, all of the Caribbean islands, and many other countries, I chose to limit my focus to Puerto Rico and Mexico because of their geographic and political ties to the United States.

This project began with the help of Boston-based journalist Twig Mowatt, a board member of Save A Sato. It was Twig who had written the article I had read a number of years ago. She educated me about the situation in Puerto Rico, answered a million nagging questions, and helped me make contacts on the island that would be invaluable in the making of *Street Dogs*. I soon realized just how overwhelming the stray dog problem is there. Although the actual number is unknowable, the small island of Puerto Rico is estimated to have between 200,000 and 300,000 dogs roaming the streets, beaches, jungles, and dumps, often in packs, looking for food, shelter, and fresh water. Many independent animal rescue groups on the island, such as

Save A Sato and Amigos de los Animales (both nonprofit organizations), are working around the clock to make a difference. Most are united with groups and shelters in the U.S. that regularly take in shipments of healthy, rehabilitated *satos* and find them new homes in the States.

My initial reaction to this information was mixed. I was relieved that so many dogs were being saved, but confused as to why the United States was taking in dogs from other countries when many of its own shelters are so overcrowded. The answer, however, is quite logical. As anyone who has ever worked or volunteered at a shelter will tell you, there is always a waiting list for puppies and small dogs. Most people wanting a small dog or young puppy do not suddenly change their minds and adopt a large shepherd or even a medium-sized terrier. They will either wait, hoping their applications are picked from the dozens submitted, or just go out and buy a dog if none is available at the shelters. Furthermore, because of location or, often, highly successful regional spay/neuter campaigns, there are a number of shelters in New England, upstate New York, and other areas that often don't have many dogs to adopt out; bringing in stray dogs from neighboring countries is a response to this need.

Small purebred dogs are very popular in Puerto Rico. When these dogs end up on the street, either lost or abandoned by their owners, the *satos* that are produced from frequent breeding are often small as well. The rescue groups that send dogs to the United States usually focus on puppies and smaller breeds because they fly out of the adoption centers. The quicker they are adopted out, the sooner more dogs can be rescued.

I left for Puerto Rico immediately after New Year, armed with stripped-down digital camera gear, too few short-sleeved shirts, and a distinct fear of what I was about to witness. Looking back, I'm glad that I began this journey in Puerto Rico. The three weeks I spent there exposed me to the worst possible scenarios in dog rescue, but I was also fortunate enough to meet and work with some of the most inspiring people imaginable. Many of these rescuers are single-handedly, and with no financial assistance from the government, saving thousands of dogs every year.

Elizabeth Kracht, who volunteered to act as my daily guide and assistant in San Juan, is an American who came to the island in 2005 to open a vitamin and health-food store with her boyfriend. As an animal lover, she was overwhelmed by the number of strays. She began researching options and networking with organizations, because, as she put it, "knowing myself, I knew I needed to

Opposite: Rescuer Steve McGarva coaxes Sadie out of the den she made for her three puppies in the jungle of Yabucoa, Puerto Rico.

prepare … it was just going to be a matter of time before I'd be in a position of not knowing what to do with an animal." Two years later, rescue has taken on a full-time role in Elizabeth's life. She and Christine Driscoll (cofounder of Amigos de los Animales Puerto Rico) escorted me to every corner of the island—through city streets, jungles, backyards, and villages—facilitating meetings and rescues and helping establish the networks that formed the fabric of this book.

In the fall of 2006, Elizabeth had received a pleading email about a beach in Yabucoa at the southeastern corner of Puerto Rico that locals have nicknamed "Dead Dog Beach." An American athlete and sculptor named Steve McGarva discovered the beach near his home after relocating to the area with his wife, who works for a pharmaceutical company. Since then, he had taken on daily feedings of dozens and dozens of dogs. He also began documenting each dog that he saw. Often he was forced to administer amateur emergency veterinary care, such as stitching wounds and setting broken bones, and to bury deceased dogs. Steve was desperate for help as he recounted the horrific things many of these dogs had endured. The atrocities ranged from abandonment to severe abuse and torture: a litter of puppies and their mother had been run over purposely by teenagers; a male dog had so much hot oil thrown over him that his organs were exposed; another dog had been hacked with a machete; and many dogs had been found dead, poisoned by fishermen, oil-company employees, and hotel staff.

By the time I got to Puerto Rico in January, Steve and Elizabeth, aided by a team of rescuers that included Mary Eldergill and Christine, had managed to take in and rehabilitate almost ninety dogs from the 1–2 square-mile beachfront wasteland. Sadly, the number of dogs keeps replenishing itself as more and more animals are dumped there daily.

On the day I toured Dead Dog Beach, we saw at least fifty strays divided into approximately three different packs. All the dogs, except for very recent newcomers, know and love Steve. When his truck comes rumbling down the rural side road leading to the beach, they come running out of the jungle and overgrowth to meet him, tails wagging. The dogs in each pack vary from small to large, mutt to purebred, aged to infant, and healthy to quite sick. Almost all are friendly and, despite their experiences, eager for human affection.

Dogs are one of the two most common domesticated animals in the world (an estimated 60 million are kept as pets in the United States alone), yet, ultimately, they are pack animals.

In the absence of structured, human lives, they act innately to fulfill one of their strongest instincts—to seek out the safety and comfort of other dogs. Although this is common knowledge among dog enthusiasts, few people ever get to witness the fascinating and intricate psychological workings of an organic pack. But at Dead Dog Beach a very obvious pecking order was clearly on display, with the most dominant dogs emerging as pack leaders. There were alpha and omega dogs as well as hierarchies involving various forms of behavior, including eating and care-giving ("surrogate mothers," "children," and "outcasts" were all evident in the pack).

One of the most touching dog stories I have ever heard involves a pack at Dead Dog Beach. On at least two occasions, Steve was physically threatened by thugs in Yabucoa (once with a machete), but was saved when alpha dog Shep (page 96) and his pack came to the rescue by forming a barricade between Steve and his attackers. The dogs growled and snapped until the men were finally driven off and Steve was able to escape.

At one point during our day at Dead Dog Beach, we heard a faint barking coming from thick jungle. After searching for about fifteen minutes, we found a very small, beige stray defending a den of sorts. She was obviously nursing, but there was no sign of her puppies. Finally we saw a little head poke out from deep in the earth. Steve befriended the nervous mother, who eventually abandoned her ferocity and collapsed into his arms. She appeared to have been dumped at pregnancy and was therefore new to life in the wild. Slowly, Elizabeth and my husband, Jesse, coaxed three healthy puppies out of an amazingly complex subterranean den built out of fallen palm trees and earth. A few days later, Sadie, as she was named, and her pups were sponsored by Save A Sato and brought to its shelter. They now all have homes in the United States.

Opposite, left: The caretaker at the Fajardo dump in Puerto Rico with Lucy. Although he could not give a home to any of the many dogs living at the dump, or afford to get them medical care, he was tolerant and kind to them.

Opposite, right: Sadie has blood drawn to test for heartworm at the Save A Sato shelter in San Juan, Puerto Rico.

One of the more frustrating experiences during my work in Puerto Rico was seeing beautiful, friendly, or ill dogs that we were not able to take off the streets because there was no funding for them. Each dog requires vet care (including spaying or neutering), boarding during their recovery, and the airfare to the States. Some dogs are kept for only a week or two, while others require months of care. Because of the high rate of abuse and abandonment, most rescue groups will not adopt

dogs out within Puerto Rico, which is why the airfare is required. Sponsors are often found to pay for a dog's rescue and rehabilitation. The initial amount required to get a dog off the streets ranges from $125 to $200. During the shooting of this book, we were fortunate enough to receive generous donations that allowed me to witness and assist in the rescue of about ten dogs from different areas in Puerto Rico.

Occasionally, larger dogs are rescued and sent to breed-specific rescues or to shelters that simply don't have many dogs. But the United States has no general shortage of medium and large homeless dogs, so it is harder to find willing sponsors for them. From time to time, however, rescuers meet a larger dog in desperate need of help and simply can't turn their backs.

There are specific reasons for the widespread abandonment of dogs that takes place in Puerto Rico. The traditional government-run pounds are overcrowded, underfunded, and seen as little more than killing facilities, so when a pet is unwanted, people turn it out on the streets, many believing that they are giving the animal at least some chance of survival. Yet the reality is that they are often condemning the dog to a slow death from disease, abuse, or being hit by a car. People are slowly beginning to realize that there are alternatives.

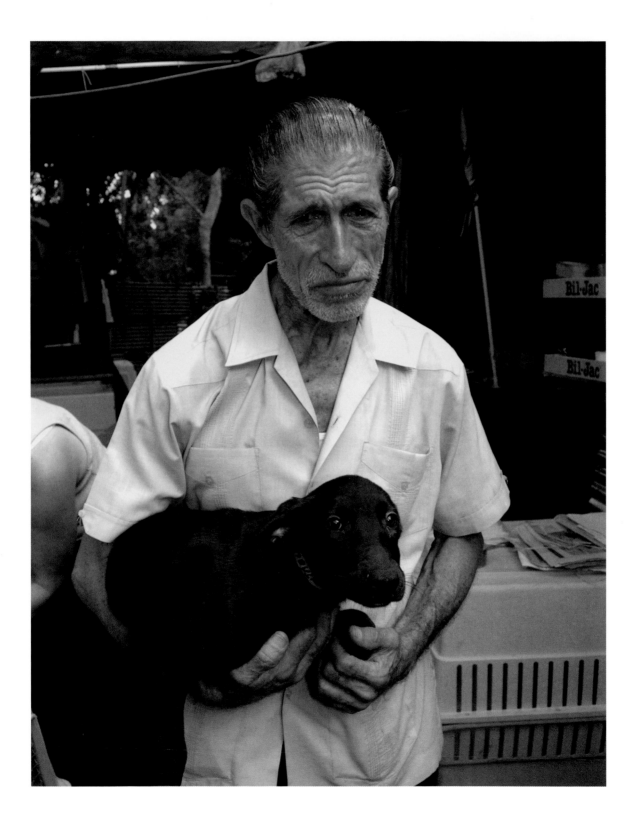

Although the municipal pounds have changed little over the years, there is hope that help will come from the private sector. The Humane Society of Puerto Rico (HSPR) is a donation-funded facility that aims to improve all aspects of companion animal welfare. In 2005 alone, it vaccinated more than 21,000 animals, sterilized about 7000, and provided low- or no-cost clinical services to over 6000 others. Each year, its number of adoptions rises, thanks in part to a very progressive promotional campaign aimed at encouraging Puerto Ricans to value "mutts" as much as purebreds. Vivid, fashionable posters and bumper stickers display the slogan *Todos somos satos, adopta una* ("We are all mutts, adopt one"). Executive director Ernesto Cruz-Feliciano is successfully using his vision and deep understanding of Puerto Rican culture to insure that HSPR becomes a visible and amiable force within the community.

The privately funded Save A Sato (SAS) is the Puerto Rican rescue group that is probably most familiar to Americans, and it sends thousands of rescued dogs every year to shelters in the U.S. I visited the SAS shelter one morning as they were preparing a shipment of dogs for the airport. The expanse of kennels is situated behind director Gloria Marti's family home in San Juan. Volunteers, well versed in the process, were tagging, recording, and crating two dozen dogs that would be flown to the States and then met at the airport by shelter workers. This procedure is often repeated several times a week, making room for the never-ending stream of dogs in need.

On this particular day, a Puerto Rican man named Felix Schmidt and his wife, Emilia Jiménez, were helping prepare the dogs for their journey. After someone explained to Mr. Schmidt that I was there shooting a book about street dogs, he began desperately trying to communicate to me. He wanted a copy of the book and hoped to see "his dogs" in it. I discovered that he and his wife had rescued a mother and four puppies from a riverbed near their home. They had fostered and raised the young puppies, which were then four months old and ready to be sent to the U.S. The mother was still in their care, along with several other family dogs.

Opposite: Puerto Rican Felix Schmidt is heartbroken as he puts one of the pups he rescued into a crate bound for the United States.

Mr. Schmidt kept trying to give me a piece of paper that I soon realized was a handwritten letter that he insisted should be sent along with each of the four puppies. Few things have ever touched me as deeply as this letter (see page 22), which detailed, in awkward but coherent English, the puppies' history and preferences, along with Mr. Schmidt's deep affection for them and his desire to establish contact with their new "parents" in the United States.

The letter began

"Hi, my name is Lucero and I am an abandoned puppy from San Juan, Puerto Rico. I wandered the streets and other areas looking for food, water, shelter and love, but I found none. My former owner put me away together with my mother and three (3) of my brothers. I do not know the real reason. ... My rescuers promised me that I will go to a wonderful place in the United States of America, where I will find a wonderful, wonderful home. I have waited patiently, and at last, I am on my way. ... I am a very sweet puppy, in spite of all that I have suffered. If you give me an opportunity you will not be sorry. I will be a very faithful pet and will give you lots of love. ... My foster parents do not keep us with them due to the fact that they have other dogs that have lived with them for many years. They felt very sad for our separation from them. If you please, I will appreciate very much if you write to them ..."

When he went to put the last puppy in a crate, Mr. Schmidt broke down in tears, clutching the dog in his arms. Lucero (page 90) and his brothers were sent to a shelter in Fort Lauderdale, where they were all adopted. I met Mr. Schmidt on one of my last days in Puerto Rico. The experience punctuated my time on the island and left me with a much-needed sense of optimism for the future of the country's dogs.

My first stop in Mexico was at the beautiful colonial city of Guanajuato. I was drawn there by an active rescue group also called Amigos de los Animales (there are several different rescue groups throughout the world with that same name). My first observation was how few dogs I saw on the streets. Director Sandra Ward and a small board of directors, comprised of both Mexicans and Americans, have made an enormous impact on the number and condition of strays in their area.

Although the group does facilitate rescues on a case-by-case basis, it believes that it is the government's responsibility to build a humane shelter. The primary focus of Amigos, therefore, is sterilization and education. Each year, it picks a particular village or region in need and hosts a huge spay/neuter campaign. Residents are strongly encouraged to participate, and the cost is kept exceedingly low. Even if some of the dogs end up back on the streets, they are unable to produce further generations of unwanted animals. Amigos has also distributed hundreds of copies of

Opposite, left: While being treated for sarcoptic mange, which is highly contagious, these puppies are kept in a kennel at the Save A Sato shelter.

Opposite, right: Gloria Marti holds up a puppy at the airport. He and his littermates were leaving Puerto Rico for a U.S. shelter.

an educational coloring book for young children entitled *Give a Hand to Animals* and a short story for older children called *Diary of an Abandoned Dog*.

On my first day at the rescue group, Sandra was showing me around when we stopped to photograph a number of healthy, well-fed strays hanging out near a fast-food stand in a small shopping plaza. A pitiful, lactating female dog attempted to get close to the stand but was chased away immediately by the pack of larger dogs. We decided to follow her, hoping that she would lead us to her puppies. She finally stopped high on a hill inside the compound of a mechanic's shop. We found her nursing nine puppies outside a den obscured from view by a tangle of brush and bushes.

Sandra and fellow Amigos rescuer James Pyle talked to the shop owner and discovered that he considered the mother to be his dog but would allow Amigos to have her spayed and adopt out the puppies. In such circumstances, if it is not possible to take the mother and the entire litter all at once, it's usually best to remove a few puppies at a time—mother dogs can suffer severe anxiety and depression if separated abruptly from their whole litter. We took three puppies

during my stay, and then Sandra went back twice more for the rest. The situation was typical of my experiences in Mexico, which were that people were often willing to embrace an alternative for their animals when presented with one.

From Guanajuato, I traveled by bus to the nearby hilly, picturesque town of San Miguel de Allende, a very popular tourist destination for Americans. There I met some of the dedicated staff and volunteers at the Sociedad Protectora de Animales (SPA), a private "no-kill" shelter that was started almost twenty years ago. One unfortunate inevitability faced by all no-kill facilities is that eventually they run out of room. They are then forced to turn dogs away, or to create a waiting list for people wishing to surrender animals. Although the SPA has a very successful adoption rate overall, I met many beautiful dogs there that had been waiting for a home for several years. These dogs were not crippled, or sick, or mangy. They were all gorgeous, healthy dogs that, because of their "common" markings or mixed heritage, were not at all distinctive and were therefore difficult to place in Mexico. When I see such dogs as Callita (page 109), Kaya (page 57), and Panga (page 26), I can't help but think how quickly they would be snapped up in the United States. (Incidentally, bringing a dog into the U.S. from Mexico is surprisingly easy, especially by car. Often all you need is proof of current vaccinations.)

In Guanajuato and San Miguel de Allende I saw far fewer street dogs than I'd anticipated, which is both a good and a bad sign. It is undoubtedly an indication of success, of which each rescue and activist group should be very proud. However, in many Mexican towns, especially those with high rates of tourism, stray dogs are frequently rounded up and killed to keep the population down and prevent tourists from seeing or being bothered by skinny, hungry animals. In Guanajuato there were a number of veteran street dogs that had won favor or familiarity with the locals and were simply allowed to be. Although they lived off scraps and handouts, most were quite well fed and unobtrusive. These are the fortunate ones.

San Felipe, in Baja California, western Mexico, presented a sharp visual and logistical contrast to the cities in the state of Guanajuato. San Felipe is a small fishing port with a unique topography. Miles of beautiful beaches on the pristine Sea of Cortez are flanked by mountains and endless desert. The town, although still very small (there is only one main road), is slowly becoming popular with American retirees. Jennifer Holmes, a New England native, moved to the area after her retirement but found a new direction in animal rescue. She is the director of the San Felipe Animal Rescue (SFAR), which was housing around a hundred homeless dogs at the time of my visit. There are an estimated 5000 stray dogs in this rural area.

Most weekends Jennifer braves a five-hour drive across the Mexican border to Arizona, where she holds adoption clinics at PetSmart stores. Once they are healthy, vaccinated, and sterilized, all adoptable dogs from SFAR are taken to Arizona to find new homes. The group also participates in the capture of wild dogs. Often, feral dogs are trapped, sterilized, treated for disease, and then released, then given access to feeding stations in their area. This not only helps move the rescue group toward its goal of zero population growth, but also insures that even "unadoptable" dogs receive medical care and basic staples.

Every day that I was in San Felipe, Jennifer and I got up at dawn, climbed into her 4x4 and rambled across unpaved, bumpy desert roads in search of an elusive pack that had been spotted several times. We never found them, but did

Opposite, left: A dog is brought into the veterinary clinic at the Sociedad Protectora de Animales in San Miguel de Allende, Mexico.

Opposite, right: Sandra Ward of Amigos de los Animales takes puppies from a junkyard in Guanajuato, Mexico.

see dozens of other dogs that would emerge only in the coolness of the early morning and twilight hours. On my last day there, we decided to track down a fenced-in lot where a large number of dogs had been sighted. The land belonged to a woman who had been suspected many times of animal hoarding. Apparently, she had been very defensive and often aggressive with anyone from SFAR who tried to intervene with her dogs.

The scene in this lot was overwhelming. A huge pack of between fifteen and twenty-five wild dogs were living there, many coming and going throughout the day via large gaps in the fence. The dogs seemed to receive food on a semi-regular basis and had therefore begun congregating there, finding shelter under a wooden dog house and some deliberately placed construction debris. There was a mother dog with ten sickly, emaciated puppies whose bellies were distended with worms. Every single dog there was terrified of humans and would not approach us at all, except in bursts of frightened aggression. It became clear that although someone was feeding these animals periodically, no one was caring for them.

Above: Puppies at the
San Felipe Animal Rescue
in Mexico.

Initially, I hovered around the perimeter of the fence, taking photos and trying to coax curious puppies over to me. The alpha males in the pack kept circling me, barking and growling incessantly but not daring to come closer than 10 feet (3 m) or so. Jennifer and I were unsure at first whether the landowner lived nearby or not, and didn't want to risk being arrested for trespassing or, worse, getting shot at. After a few phone calls, Jennifer discovered that the woman lived miles away, so I decided to go under the fence in order to get more photos and try to capture some of the sickest puppies. The minute I entered the enclosure, the level of aggression increased, but when I put food down, it escalated into a full-scale frenzy. I handed one screaming, thrashing puppy over the fence to Jennifer, who put him in her truck and then entered the property herself. She managed to grab two puppies and then headed for a hole in the fence just as I was struggling to wrench another one away from the increasingly angry pack. I turned around to see Jennifer stuck in the cactus fence, still grasping the puppies, with two males attacking her on both sides. When I turned back to struggle with the hissing puppy sliding out of my hold, a male grabbed the back of my leg and bit down hard. I dropped the puppy (regrettably) and slowly backed up until I reached the fence.

I have never been attacked like this by a dog. In retrospect, I think it was pure arrogance to assume that I wouldn't be. These dogs were wild, but unlike many, had a small, well-defined, enclosed territory to guard, which I believe made them much more aggressive than wild dogs that can simply escape by running further into the desert or jungle or maze of city streets.

Back at SFAR, we assessed our wounds, and I became hugely grateful for having worn thick jeans, which had saved me from losing a valuable piece of my calf. While we were cleaning our bites, the three terrified puppies managed to escape from the back of Jennifer's truck. We had no choice but to terrorize them further by capturing all three for the second time in one day. They put up an impressive fight for such tiny, weak animals. My heart went out to them. There was no way for them to understand that we were trying to help. For all they knew, our actions were an indication that we were about to eat them.

Fortunately, this incident took place on my last day of travel for *Street Dogs*. One long car ride, a two-hour bus trip, several cabs, and two flights later, I was home with my family, trying to process all that I had witnessed in the past two months. I could write volumes recounting endless anecdotes and stories of success, heartbreak, exhilaration, and exhaustion that I, and the people who worked so harmoniously with me, experienced during the making

JANUARY 15, 2007
TO MY NEW OWNERS:

HI, MY NAME IS LUCERO AND I AM AN ABANDONED PUPPY FROM SAN JUAN, PUERTO RICO. I WANDERED THE STREETS AND OTHER AREAS, LOOKING FOR FOOD, WATER, SHELTER AND LOVE, BUT I FOUND NONE. MY FORMER OWNER PUT ME AWAY TOGETHER WITH MY MOTHER AND THREE (3) OF MY BROTHERS. I DO NOT KNOW THE REAL REASON. WE SURVIVED ON MERE SCRAPS AND ON ANYTHING THAT HAD A SLIGHT SMELL OF FOOD.

ONE DAY WE MET A LOVELY COUPLE (FOSTER FATHERS) NAMED FÉLIX SCHMIDT AND EMILIA JIMÉNEZ, WHO TOOK PITY OF US AND RESCUED US FROM OUR MISERY. HE (F.S.) AND HIS WIFE (E.J.) WERE VERY LOVING TO US TOWARD US AND TOOK US TO THEIR HOME, WHERE THEY TOOK WON-DERFUL CARE OF US.

MY RESCUERS PROMISED ME THAT I WILL GO TO A WONDERFUL PLACE IN THE UNITED STATES OF AMERICA, WHERE I WILL FIND A WONDERFUL, WONDERFUL HOME. I HAVE WAITED PATIENTLY, AND AT LAST, I AM ON MY WAY.

I AM A VERY SWEET PUPPY, IN SPITE OF ALL THAT I HAVE SUFFERED. IF YOU GIVE ME AN OPPORTUINITY YOU WILL NOT BE SORRY. I WILL BE A VERY FAITHFUL PET AND WILL GIVE YOU LOTS OF LOVE.

— OVER —

of this book. But in the end, it is the job of the photographs to communicate what I can't even begin to explain in words.

Street Dogs attempts to raise awareness of a battle that will ultimately be won through education, legislation, and dedication. But it also celebrates the pure, unbreakable spirit of the dog—trusting, kind, and playful, despite injury, abuse, and hardship. There are few motives behind the affection of a dog. I have witnessed packs of starving, diseased, and discarded dogs come running joyfully to me. They stayed, even when I didn't have any food. No matter what, they desperately want to love us, and we owe it to them to show compassion in return.

Although there is some practical truth in the saying "first the people, then the animals," if followed blindly, it becomes a mantra of apathy and avoidance. Compassion is a key element of being human and does not dictate that you should choose between feeding your child or feeding your dog, nor does it condone violence or abuse from the abused and beaten. "Caring" for an animal means something different to everyone. For some, it means gourmet kibble, day care, and dressing dogs in frilly sweaters, but at the most basic level it simply involves kindness. Dogs are remarkably capable of being happy with very little. A safe environment, an affectionate caress, and scraps from the kitchen go a long way.

Alternatives to abandonment and neglect, as well as low- or no-cost sterilization and vet care, are now available in many places where previously there were few options. Humane education is beginning to reach into elementary schools in Mexico, Puerto Rico, and many other countries, where old myths and prejudices are being re-evaluated and children are being taught to value all life. Leaders follow leaders. I have witnessed both compassion and cruelty from people of all walks of life, but one thing I noticed acutely in producing this book was that there were many people who did want to care, they just didn't know how.

As with most waves of social change, small, dedicated groups of individuals are beginning to make an enormous impact, both directly and on the collective consciousness in many towns. A global synergy is taking place. All over the world, geographically scattered but ethically united rescuers and educators are ushering in a new era of compassion and kindness toward the animals with whom we share our lives. This is true grassroots activism in its purest form and should serve to inspire anyone who thinks that one person cannot make a difference.

Opposite: Mr. Schmidt's letter to the American adopters of Lucero, one of the puppies he rescued.

STREETdogs

amber

panga

A litter of puppies comes out from under an old car to eat kibble put down by volunteers in Guanajuato, Mexico.

*A Guanajuato street dog hangs out in front
of a busy restaurant in search of food.*

*A female member of a pack in San Felipe, Mexico, tries to nudge a puppy back
into the safety of its den. For more details on these dogs, see page 53.*

sadie

canela

peanut

buddy

A stray in Guanajuato, Mexico, rests on the sunny sidewalk of a busy downtown street. I met this friendly cocker spaniel inside the mercado *(market), where he searches for scraps of meat. He followed me around for an hour, always trailing a few feet behind.*

*Three strays sit in the shade under
the palm trees that line Dead Dog
Beach in Yabucoa, Puerto Rico.*

A scrawny mother nurses her litter of puppies. We found her looking for scraps in the parking lot of a movie theater. Noticing her milk, we followed her a few blocks back to her den on the side of a steep hill, next to an auto shop in Guanajuato, Mexico. The owner of the shop claimed that she was his dog but allowed Amigos de los Animales to adopt out her puppies and have her spayed.

A well-fed stray, Chow, known all around
Guanajuato, takes a nap on the street
in front of the city's police.

heather

sugar

smiley

The most amazing part of rescuing dogs
off the streets is the ability they have
to love, and the devotion that they possess
even when they are suffering. They still
have love and gentleness in their eyes.
When I go up to the States and find
a home for one of the dogs who came to
us half-dead, I have this wonderful feeling
of complete connection, and in my soul
I know that this is what I am meant to do.

Jennifer Holmes, San Felipe Animal Rescue, Mexico

Wolly and Onyx run after our truck as we approach the San Felipe Animal Rescue in Mexico. Both dogs were once housed in the rescue center but kept breaking out to run free in the neighborhood during the day. At night, they sleep curled up together on a special bed put out for them in the center's sandy parking lot. They are inseparable.

*Wolly and Onyx chase our car
in San Felipe, Mexico.*

*A friendly dog greets us at dawn in the middle
of a desert road in San Felipe.*

elsa

lulabelle

I took a chance and adopted
a badly abused, seriously neglected
young dog. Yet the dog is as affectionate,
loyal, and delightful as if we'd raised her
from a puppy with never a harsh word.
Baggage? Resentment? Not a bit of it.
Just gratitude and unconditional love.
So I say with some confidence,
take a chance on a street dog.

Christine Foster, Sociedad Protectora de
Animales de San Miguel de Allende, Mexico

Chow Chow

A middle-aged female in San Felipe, Mexico, acts as a protector to a litter of puppies while their mother is busy eating. This white female would stand stiffly between me and the puppies each time I tried to photograph them in their den under the porch. When the curious puppies toddled out to see me, she would nudge them back under the porch and pace nervously until their mother returned.

Rescuer Jennifer Holmes and I chased these two stray males through the desert in San Felipe, Mexico, determined to win them over. Eventually I followed them on foot. When the white dog began to give in to the urge to approach me, I laid down on my back in an attempt to demonstrate submissiveness. He was immediately very affectionate, while his wary Doberman friend remained about 20 feet (6 m) away from me.

A beautiful street dog waits for handouts at the entrance to an urban mercado in Guanajuato, Mexico. This recent mother was very shy and sweet. She returned to the same market every day, quietly hoping for scraps.

kaya

charmin

56

beauty

miss trish

This watchful dog was the alpha male of a pack of five adult dogs that were found living in an abandoned beachfront property in San Felipe, Mexico. The former tenant and owner of the dogs had disappeared more than two months before this photo was shot. Rescuer Jennifer Holmes had taken over daily feedings of the dogs and was working to bring each one into the shelter.

A feral puppy runs from us at the dump
near San Miguel de Allende, Mexico. A huge
pack of dogs lives at the dump site and on
its surrounding land, feeding off garbage.
All the dogs we encountered at the
dump were terrified of people.

A street dog in Guanajuato,
Mexico, waits outside a bakery
for handouts.

A dog emerges to take a look at
us at dawn on a desert road
in San Felipe, Mexico.

*A plucky, stray shar-pei trots down the
cobblestoned streets of Guanajuato, Mexico.*

*A young street dog yawns on the
steps of a monument in Guanajuato.*

lobo

muffin

One of the more sickly members of a feral litter found in a lot ventured through the fence for a better look at us. He was rescued that night and taken to the San Felipe Animal Rescue, Mexico, where he was affectionately named Gremlin because of the way he screamed and hissed when we tried to take him.

A very friendly, well-fed, stray pit bull comes up to see me on the street.
This guy is well known locally in San Juan, Puerto Rico, for hanging out
every night in front of Pippin's restaurant, where the employees feed him.
One night I saw him waiting to cross an extremely busy four-lane road.
The next day, he was back on this sidewalk near Pippin's.

A young street dog searches for food behind a house in Marfil, Mexico. Like so many strays, she had the chewed remnants of a rope tied around her neck. She quickly warmed to me, and soon laid her head in my lap. Sandra Ward of Amigos de los Animales was determined to help me bring her back to the United States, and she watched the area for days after this shot was taken, but never saw her again.

A young stray hangs around a traditional kiosko (kiosk) in Piñones, Puerto Rico, at sunset.

Three strays congregate around us in Santa Ana, Mexico. Rescuer Sandra Ward had cheese and tortillas on hand for all of them.

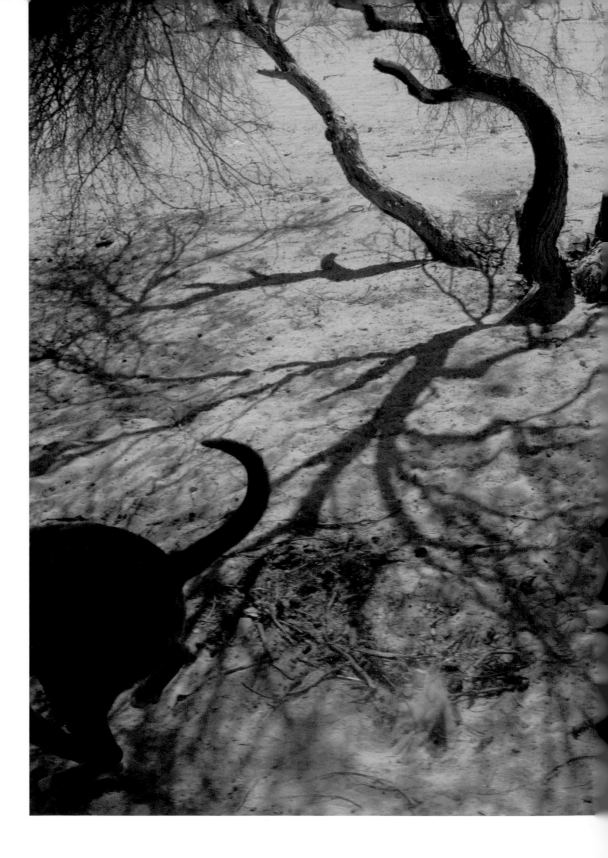

Two dogs enjoy a run in San Felipe, Mexico.

coco

faye

A street dog in Guanajuato, Mexico, follows a couple
through a public square, hoping for a handout.

A well-fed Guanajuato street dog naps
at the entrance to a souvenir store.

This stray dog ran nervously
on to the roof of a house in
Piñones, Puerto Rico, when
we approached.

*Puerto Rican beach-stray
Sally, a few days before she
was rescued by Christine
Driscoll and her husband,
Carlos. Middle-aged Sally
was treated for heartworm,
dehydration, and various
other conditions before
being adopted by
a local man.*

*A curious puppy comes to the fence
of the vacant lot where she and her
siblings live with their mother and
numerous other strays.*

A newly arrived street dog pauses outside the Puerto Rican beachfront hotel he had been hanging around for a few weeks. Rescuer Elizabeth Kracht and I tried to coax him into a crate, but he became fearful and darted off down the street. Sadly, a week later, he was hit by a car, suffered a fractured spine, and had to be euthanized.

A litter of puppies huddles together at dusk in San Felipe, Mexico. The puppies, along with their mother and a dozen other wild dogs, lived together as a pack in a fenced-in lot, where they had some shelter and were fed occasionally by the landowner. A number of the puppies were sick, and we took in three of them on the day this photo was taken. While trying to get one of the screaming, frightened pups out of the lot, Jennifer Holmes and I were both attacked by separate alpha male dogs.

A stray lies in the shady jungle surrounding Dead Dog Beach in Yabucoa, Puerto Rico.

pinta

lucrecia

daryl

lucero

A pack of friendly strays living at the
Fajardo dump in Puerto Rico perks up
at the sight of our car.

Two puppies, part of a larger pack that lives
on Los Machos beach in Puerto Rico, seek
comfort from each other. They were later taken
in by rescuer Mary Eldergill and eventually
adopted out of the island through St. Hubert's
Animal Welfare in New Jersey.

An old, cancer-ridden, male street dog patrols the parking lot of Amigo supermarket in Salinas, Puerto Rico, hoping for scraps. When we came to give the dogs their food and water, we were harassed by a store security guard, who insisted we should not encourage the dogs to stay by feeding them. He said it was bad for business.

*A beautiful stray puppy follows us hesitantly
down the street in Santa Ana, Mexico.*

*Rescue organizations alone
are left responsible, financially
and otherwise, for bringing
Puerto Rico into the present,
where the humane treatment
of animals is the only option.*

Elizabeth Kracht, Amigos de los Animales Puerto Rico

shep

simpatica

gumdrop

I started rescuing dogs when I was living in Mexico. I would take them to the vet and then foster them at my house until I could find them a home. When I moved here to Puerto Rico about eleven years ago, I was shocked at the number of stray dogs, cats, and even horses that I saw. I started rescuing dogs here almost immediately after I arrived. I was completely broke, but spent every last penny on veterinary bills. Over the years, I was lucky enough to meet other people who were doing the same thing. Eventually I officially formed the nonprofit Amigos de los Animales, Inc.

Christine Driscoll, founder, Amigos de los Animales Puerto Rico

A pack runs together at the
Fajardo dump in Puerto Rico.

Benji, a sweet, dreadlocked stray at Dead Dog Beach, Puerto Rico, licks his chops after a treat from U.S. tugboat operators (seen here with rescuer Steve McGarva, far right). About a month after my visit, Benji was found beaten to death. He had been the next in line to be rescued from the beach.

A dog stands in the jungle at Dead Dog Beach, waiting for food from rescuers.

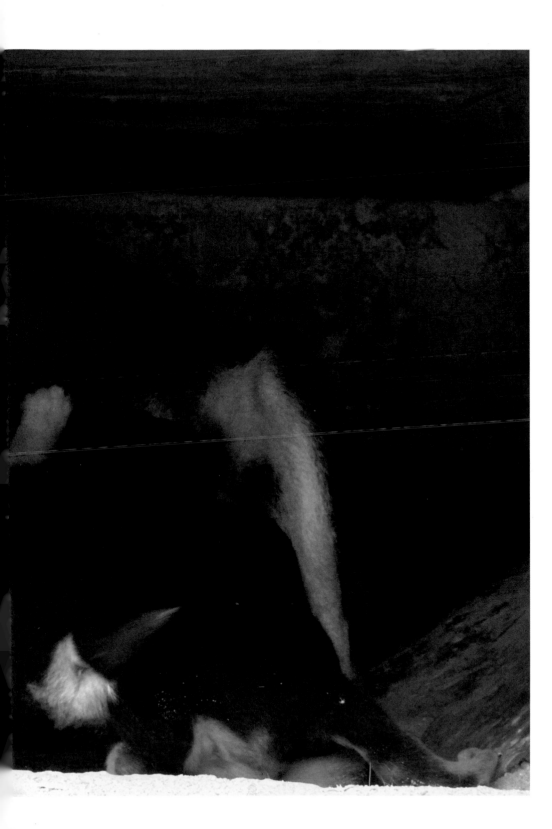

A mother and her very healthy five-week-old puppies were found living with four other adult dogs at an abandoned house in San Felipe, Mexico (see page 53). Mom and pups were taken to the San Felipe Animal Rescue.

skippy

callita

buddy

poca

Two puppies emerge from under a car in San
Felipe, Mexico, to take a closer look at us.

A veteran street dog lounges in front of a small store in Marfil,
Mexico. This male had previously been caught, neutered, and released
by Amigos de los Animales. The scars on his face are the result of his
propensity for instigating territorial brawls with other dogs.

A stray on the beach in
Piñones, Puerto Rico, hovers
quietly near two girls.

A street dog in Guanajuato, Mexico, looks for water.

A relaxed stray in Guanajuato
sleeps through the afternoon heat in
the shade of a crowded bus stop.

A weak, injured puppy hides near a large

truck at the dump in Fajardo, Puerto Rico.

A young dog tries to stay cool by digging out a hole in the sand under a shady palm tree at Dead Dog Beach in Puerto Rico.

jess

A wonderful beach dog in San Felipe adopted me, which made me realize how many more animals there were in need. He opened my eyes to the animal humane needs of this poor Baja fishing community.

Ronda Walpole, founder, San Felipe Animal Rescue, Mexico

Who's Who

Amber, page 27. Brought to rescuer Mary Eldergill by the mother of a Puerto Rican beauty queen, three-month-old Amber and her sister had been found on the side of the road. Amber is what Mary calls a "weak specimen," having had many health problems in her short life. She would not have survived on her own and after her rescue spent weeks on an intravenous drip.

Beauty, page 58. Rescued by a veterinarian from the Mexico City pound, Beauty was pregnant and facing euthanasia. She was brought to the San Felipe Animal Rescue, where she delivered her litter. The puppies were small and weak, and all but one of them died of distemper. The remaining puppy was nursed back to health by rescuer Jennifer Holmes and was later adopted out in Arizona.

Buddy (Labrador mix), page 35. One of San Felipe Animal Rescue's first dogs, Buddy has been at the shelter for five years because he has never completely regained his health. The distemper from which he suffered as a puppy gives his nose the appearance of rubber. Buddy is considered a "lifer" and will spend the rest of his years lounging in the compound of the San Felipe Animal Rescue.

Buddy (terrier mix), page 111. Rescued from a dam in the mountains of Puerto Rico, where he lived with a pack of other strays, Buddy has never got over his debilitating fear of humans. He was still in foster care more than two years after his rescue.

Callita, page 109. A street dog in San Miguel de Allende, Mexico, who was spayed and released back into the neighborhood, Callita kept returning to the Sociedad Protectora de Animales. She was eventually taken in and was awaiting adoption.

Canela, page 33. Rescuers saw a posting by a woman desperate to get Canela ("cinnamon" in Spanish) and her newborn pups out of a store parking lot in Puerto Rico, where they had been living. The owner of the store had told the concerned woman that she had one week to remove the dogs or else he would poison them all. Canela and her litter were taken to a kennel. The puppies were eventually flown to the U.S. and adopted out. Canela was taken to St. Hubert's Animal Welfare in New Jersey.

Charmin, page 56. Rescued from Dead Dog Beach in Puerto Rico, Charmin was fostered and doted on by rescuer Elizabeth Kracht for three months while being treated for recurring skin problems. Although initially Charmin was scared of everything, she blossomed in foster care with the help of Elizabeth and many animal companions, including a litter of mischievous kittens. Charmin was adopted out by Tri Boro Animal Welfare in New Jersey.

Chow Chow, page 50. When he was found, in Puerto Rico, Chow Chow had been severely abused, and had a dozen cigarette burns on his back and one eye gouged out. He is famous on the island for having walked over 25 miles (40 km) back to the vet's where he had been treated, when his first adoptive family went on vacation. Soon after this he was adopted into a forever home, where he lives with his humans and two other rescue dogs.

Coco, page 77. Intelligent and beautiful, Coco (as in Coco Chanel, the French fashion designer) was found on the side of a busy road in San Felipe, Mexico, by rescuer Jennifer Holmes when she was about seven weeks old. She rode around with us in the truck for much of that day and was then brought to the San Felipe Animal Rescue, where she joined up with a small gang of rescued puppies. About three weeks later, Coco was adopted out to a new home in Arizona.

Daryl, page 91. Found by the waterfront, emaciated and with a severe case of mange, Daryl had been in recovery for eight months at the San Felipe Animal Rescue in Mexico. He was soon to be adopted out in Arizona.

Elsa, page 49. Rescued from Dead Dog Beach in Puerto Rico, Elsa was found by rescuers with her lone puppy, Yara. She was fiercely protective of her pup and kept her hidden in a damp cave. Despite suffering major health problems as a result of these living conditions, Yara survived. Happy, talkative Elsa was treated for heartworm and venereal tumors and went into foster care while awaiting a home.

Faye, page 76. One of five dogs living in an abandoned lot by the sea in San Felipe, Mexico, Faye was the pack's omega female. Rescuer Jennifer Holmes and I brought her in on my last day in San Felipe. She immediately took to riding around with us in the truck but was very intimidated by the other dogs when we arrived at the animal rescue. Faye was adopted into a new home in Arizona.

Frieda, page 2. Rescued from the street at five months old, Frieda was taken in by the Sociedad Protectora de Animales in San Miguel de Allende, Mexico. This bright, lovable dog had been waiting for more than a year for her forever home.

Gumdrop, page 101. Rescuers witnessed men in Salinas, Puerto Rico, flicking hot oil on virtually hairless, mange-ridden Gumdrop. When asked for an explanation of their behavior, they said that the dog was very ugly and they wanted her to go away. Gumdrop was treated for severe burns, heartworm, and mange. After recovering for almost a year in foster care, she was sent to St. Hubert's Animal Welfare in New Jersey.

Heather, page 40, and **Henley,** page 99. Two of six shar-pei–mix puppies. The litter's mom, Hannah, was spotted in a parking lot, very pregnant. Edi Vasquez from Save A Sato took her in, and the pups were born that night. The puppies were sent to the Sterling Animal Shelter in Massachusetts, where they found new homes. Hannah remained in foster care at Edi's home.

Jess, page 120. One of the alpha males at Dead Dog Beach in Puerto Rico, Jess was found suffering from life-threatening injuries. In an act of unfathomable cruelty, someone had poured so much hot oil on him that it had burned through his skin and left some organs exposed. In order to save his life, Steve McGarva was forced to perform emergency amateur surgery and stitch him up on the spot. The wounds have still not healed completely, and Jess is left with a massive scar stretching across one entire side of his body. After his rescue, Jess lived at a kennel facility for a year and a half until, finally, in 2007, he found his forever home with a loving family in Washington State.

Kaya, page 57. Shepherd mix Kaya was found on the streets of San Miguel de Allende, Mexico, as a puppy and brought to the Sociedad Protectora de Animales. The beautiful, now fully grown dog was waiting for a good home in Mexico or the U.S.

Lobo, page 67. Named for his resemblance to a wolf, Lobo lived for eight months as a stray in a small American neighborhood in Mexico, where he was well fed by the residents. He was taken in by the San Felipe Animal Rescue to be neutered and then found to have a sexually transmitted cancer and a glandular problem. He was neutered, treated, and released into his old neighborhood.

Lucero, page 90. Rescued from a riverbed, along with his mom and three siblings, Lucero was brought to Save A Sato, Puerto Rico, by Mr. Schmidt and his wife. The couple took care of the puppies for four months, until they were old enough to be sent to the U.S. for adoption. Mr. Schmidt cried when he put Lucero into the travel crate, despite assurances that the puppies would find a wonderful new home overseas.

Lucrecia, page 88. Found starving and completely hairless with two of her puppies and eighteen tuxedo (or bicolored) cats at a drug addict's house in San Felipe, Mexico, Lucrecia underwent treatment for many months. When her mange heals, she will be taken to Arizona for adoption.

Lulabelle, page 48. Removed temporarily from a home in Mexico where she and her litter could not be cared for, Lulabelle raised her puppies at the San Felipe Animal Rescue in Mexico. After her puppies were weaned she was ready to go back to her home—although no one had yet come to collect her.

Miss Trish, page 59. When she was found by rescuer Mary Eldergill in Salinas, Puerto Rico, Miss Trish was in heat and had heartworm. She was soon spayed and treated, and quickly became a favorite with everyone because of her humorous fanglike teeth and charming personality. Miss Trish was sent to Tri-Boro Animal Welfare in New Jersey, where she was quickly adopted.

Muffin, page 66. When Muffin was rescued from Dead Dog Beach in Puerto Rico, her fur was immediately shaved in order to treat a severe skin infection. She was initially very hostile and bit everyone who came near her in the kennel. Rescuer Mary Eldergill took her into foster care, where she was socialized and recovered both emotionally and physically. Muffin was adopted into a new home in the U.S. about three months later.

Panga, page 26. Panga and her five siblings were born at the Sociedad Protectora de Animales in San Miguel de Allende, Mexico, after their pregnant mother was brought in off the streets.

Pay, page 24. Brought to Save A Sato, Puerto Rico, as a puppy, Pay ("pie" in Spanish)—a large Dalmatian/boxer mix—was finally sent to the U.S. at one year old to find a forever home. He was housed at St. Hubert's Animal Welfare in New Jersey, where he was adored by the staff, who let him sit up-front in the reception area with them. Pay was adopted permanently by a St. Hubert's employee.

Peanut, page 34. Rescuer Elizabeth Kracht and I found Peanut gingerly following a security guard at the dump in San Juan, Puerto Rico. She was quite thin, and her belly was severely distended from worms. Peanut was very timid and wary of me when she spent her first-ever night indoors, in my apartment. The next day she joined the pack at rescuer Mary Eldergill's house. She was sent to the Humane Society of Broward County in Florida a few weeks later and was adopted into a new home.

Pinta, page 89. A lifelong stray, Pinta was discovered in a field in Mexico in 2003. She had been hit by a car and had healed on her own, leaving her crippled with a mangled "flipper" foot. Now ten years old, she lives permanently at the San Felipe Animal Rescue.

Poca, page 110. A truly unique-looking dog, Poca was found by a young Canadian tourist on the streets of San Miguel de Allende, Mexico, and brought in to the Sociedad Protectora de Animales. The young woman kept in touch with the shelter to monitor Poca's progress and posted adoption flyers for her all over the area. Despite these efforts, Poca was still awaiting a home.

Sadie, page 32. Two rescuers and I heard Sadie barking from deep in the jungle surrounding Dead Dog Beach in Puerto Rico. After an extensive search, we found her and her three pups in a remarkable den made out of palm trees and earth. The puppies were so well hidden in the chambers of the den that it took all three of us to flush them out while Sadie watched nervously. She had only recently been abandoned, and her initial fear of us melted quickly. Mother and puppies were sponsored by Save A Sato and then sent to St. Hubert's Animal Welfare in New Jersey.

Shep, page 96. Taken in from Dead Dog Beach in Puerto Rico, Shep was one of the alpha males in the pack. On at least two occasions, Shep and his pack protected rescuer Steve McGarva from violent robberies in Yabucoa by physically forcing themselves between Steve and the potential assailants. After having femur surgery and being treated for heartworm, Shep was sent to St. Hubert's Animal Welfare in New Jersey and was soon adopted.

Simpatica, page 98. After her elderly owner was put in a home, Simpatica was left uncared for in a fenced-in lot. The family then put her out on the streets, where she was stabbed multiple times in the back. Her wounds have never healed properly, which makes rehoming her impossible. She came to the San Felipe Animal Rescue in Mexico years ago and will live peacefully for the rest of her life in the shelter compound.

Skippy, page 108. Limping and emaciated, Skippy, a corgi mix, was found wandering in the rain behind a housing development in Puerto Rico. Although dirty and weak, he managed to wag his tail and allowed Save A Sato's Edi Vasquez to pick him up. He recovered in foster care but was always fearful of strangers. Skippy was sent to the Northeast Animal Shelter in Salem, Massachusetts, where he was adopted.

Smiley, page 42. Named for his tendency to bare his teeth in a "smile" when happy or excited, Smiley was found wounded in a ditch by rescuer Mary Eldergill in Salinas, Puerto Rico. He had been hit by a car and his front leg was badly broken in multiple places, so needed to be amputated. After his recovery, Smiley was sent to Tri-Boro Animal Welfare in New Jersey, where he was adopted within a few weeks.

Sugar, page 41. Sugar was found as a tiny puppy, in a cardboard box in the back of a truck in Mexico. She was emaciated, dehydrated, and very near death when the San Felipe Animal Rescue took her in. After she recovered, shelter operator Jennifer Holmes attempted to adopt her out to willing families but couldn't bear to part with her. She soon decided that Sugar was destined to be part of her own permanent pack.

Nonprofit Rescue Groups and Shelters

WORLD SOCIETY FOR THE PROTECTION OF ANIMALS (WSPA)
wspa-usa.org
wspa.ca
wspa.or.cr
wspa.org.uk
wspa-international.org
The WSPA works internationally to improve the welfare of animals and to end cruelty toward them. It achieves positive results for wildlife and companion and farm animals through fieldwork, disaster relief, education, and campaigns to improve legislation and build awareness. WSPA is recognized by the United Nations, and delivers long-term solutions by building the capacity of local organizations. By bringing together the energies of nearly 800 member organizations and people from around the world, WSPA is creating a powerful, unified animal welfare movement.

PEGASUS FOUNDATION INTERNATIONAL
pegasusfoundation.org
The Pegasus Foundation improves the welfare of wild and domestic animals in the United States, the Caribbean, on Native American lands, and in Kenya by reducing animal suffering and overpopulation, and by protecting wildlife habitats. The foundation works closely with, and helps fund, Caribbean animal welfare groups. It also works to engage tourists and solicits their financial support with assistance from the tourism industry, demonstrating tangible results of animal-related programs to tourism businesses.

Puerto Rico

AMIGOS DE LOS ANIMALES PUERTO RICO
San Juan, Puerto Rico
amigosdelosanimalespr.org
This nonprofit organization is dedicated to the rescue, rehabilitation, and rehoming of the countless abused, abandoned, and stray animals roaming Puerto Rico. It also pursues cruelty investigation, and works with the public and government officials to further animal welfare.

HUMANE SOCIETY OF PUERTO RICO (HSPR)
San Juan, Puerto Rico
hspr.org
HSPR's mission is to promote the health and welfare of animals and to work toward alleviating their suffering. It actively pursues a policy of public education directed toward the humane treatment of animals, provides low-cost sterilization and vet care, and promotes the adoption of stray and surrendered animals.

PARE ESTE, INC.
Fajardo, Puerto Rico
pareeste.org
Pare Este's goal is to raise community awareness regarding treatment of companion animals through humane education in schools, and to provide services for animals in need.

SAVE A SATO FOUNDATION (SAS)
San Juan, Puerto Rico
saveasato.org
The Save A Sato Foundation is a nonprofit organization dedicated to improving the quality of life for homeless and abused animals on the island of Puerto Rico. In the past ten years, SAS has rescued over 15,000 dogs. It operates on a solely volunteer and private donations basis.

Mexico

AMIGOS DE LOS ANIMALES DE GUANAJUATO A.C.
Guanajuato, Mexico
amigosanimalesgto.org
Amigos de los Animales de Guanajuato was formed in 2002 and is now registered in the United States as a voluntary, not-for-profit, tax-exempt association. Its mission is to reduce the suffering of street dogs and cats in the municipality of Guanajuato, Mexico.

BAJA ANIMAL SANCTUARY
Rosarito Beach, Mexico
bajaanimalsanctuary.org
Baja Animal Sanctuary is a no-kill shelter in northern Mexico that provides a safe haven for dogs and cats in need. Animals are euthanized only in cases of extreme illness.

COMPASSION WITHOUT BORDERS (CWOB)
Woodland, California, United States
cwob.org
Since 2001, Compassion Without Borders has been coordinating an international rescue from Mexico to northern California. The rescue began from the Refugio Franciscano, a large no-kill shelter in Mexico City that houses approximately 2000 animals. Since then, CWOB has expanded its effort to include dogs from animal control centers in Juarez, Mexico, where it is currently working on citywide humane reform.

REFUGIO FRANCISCANO
Mexico City, Mexico
refugiofranciscano.org
A large no-kill sanctuary that houses up to 2000 animals taken from the streets, abusive situations, and city pounds.

SAN FELIPE ANIMAL RESCUE (SFAR)
San Felipe, Mexico
sfanimalrescue.org
The SFAR aims to spay and neuter at least 70 percent of the dog population in San Felipe while also treating disease. It runs a no-kill shelter facility that provides temporary care to dogs that will be adopted out in the United States, as well as a permanent home to animals that are severely injured, sick, or unadoptable.

SOCIEDAD PROTECTORA DE ANIMALES DE SAN MIGUEL DE ALLENDE (SPA)
Guanajuato, Mexico
spasanmiguel.org
The SPA is an organization for the well-being of abandoned and homeless dogs and cats in San Miguel de Allende and environs. It runs an on-premise clinic that offers low-cost healthcare for pets owned by people of modest means. The SPA enthusiastically seeks permanent loving homes for all its resident animals.

The organizations listed here are some of the most active and vocal in their work on behalf of street dogs. A portion of the proceeds from sales of Street Dogs *will be donated to the World Society for the Protection of Animals to support work by the WSPA and its member societies to improve the welfare and reduce the suffering of street dogs in the Caribbean and Latin America. The author and publisher also wish to acknowledge the ASPCA, which is the beneficiary of a portion of the proceeds from sales of Traer Scott's first book,* Shelter Dogs.

Acknowledgments

Eternal thanks to all of the people who donated their time, talent, sponsorship, and homes to me during the making of Street Dogs: *Elizabeth Kracht, Christine Driscoll, Edi Vasquez, Jennifer Holmes, Sandra Ward, Mary Eldergill, Steve McGarva, Katherine Kerr, Adrienne Galler Lastra, Twig Mowatt, Gloria Marti, Kathy Hamblet, Christine Foster, James Pyle, Save A Sato, Amigos de los Animales de Guanajuato, and San Felipe Animal Rescue.*

First published 2007 by Merrell Publishers Limited

Head office:
81 Southwark Street
London SE1 0HX

New York office:
740 Broadway, 12th Floor
New York, NY 10003

merrellpublishers.com

Photographs copyright © 2007 Traer Scott
Text copyright © 2007 Traer Scott
Design and layout copyright © 2007 Merrell
  Publishers Limited

British Library Cataloguing-in-Publication Data:
Scott, Traer
Street dogs
1. Dogs – Pictorial works 2. Dog rescue –
Pictorial works
I. Title
636.7'00222

ISBN-13: 978-1-8589-4408-1
ISBN-10: 1-8589-4408-2

Produced by Merrell Publishers Limited
Designed by 3+Co.
Copy-edited by Diana Loxley
Proof-read by Kate Michell

Printed and bound in China

Jacket, front: Canela
Jacket, back: top left, Amber; top right, Gumdrop;
  bottom left, Shep
Page 2: Frieda
Pages 4–5: A pack of friendly strays living at a dump
  in Fajardo, Puerto Rico
Page 24: Pay
For information on all the named dogs,
  see pages 122–25.

For additional information
on Traer Scott, please visit
traerscott.com